GRASSLAND

Sean Callery

Consultant: David Burnie

KINGFISHER

NEW YORK

KINGFISHER
LONDON & NEW YORK

Copyright © Kingfisher 2011
Published in the United States by Kingfisher,
175 Fifth Ave., New York, NY 10010
Kingfisher is an imprint of Macmillan Children's Books, London.
All rights reserved.

Distributed in the U.S. by Macmillan, 175 Fifth Ave., New York, NY 10010

Library of Congress Cataloging-in-Publication data has been applied for.

ISBN: 978-0-7534-6692-6

Kingfisher books are available for special promotions and premiums.
For details contact: Special Markets Department, Macmillan,
175 Fifth Ave., New York, NY 10010.

For more information, please visit www.kingfisherbooks.com

Printed in China
1 3 5 7 9 8 6 4 2
1TR/0611/WKT/UNTD/140MA

Note to readers: the website addresses listed in this book are correct at
the time of going to print. However, due to the ever-changing nature
of the Internet, website addresses and content can change. Websites
can contain links that are unsuitable for children. The publisher cannot
be held responsible for changes in website addresses or content or for
information obtained through a third party. We strongly advise that
Internet searches should be supervised by an adult.

The publisher would like to thank the following for permission to reproduce their material. Every care has been taken to trace copyright holders. However, if there have been unintentional omissions or failure to trace copyright holders, we apologize and will, if informed, endeavor to make corrections in any future edition.
top = t; bottom = b; center = c; left = l; right = r

All artwork Stuart Jackson-Carter (Peter Kavanagh Art Agency)

Cover tl Shutterstock/Francois van Heerden; cover tl Shutterstock/jele; cover tr Shutterstock/Stephen Meese; cover tr Shutterstock/photobar; cover c Shutterstock/Justin Black; back cover cl Shutterstock/Roger Meerts; back cover c Shutterstock/P. Schwarz; back cover bc Shutterstock/Elena Butinova; 1 Shutterstock/pix2go; 2 Shutterstock/Larsek; 3t Shutterstock/FloridaStock; 3b Shutterstock/Hugh Lansdown; 4t Shutterstock/James Thew; 4bl Photolibrary/Imagestate; 4bc Shutterstock/Sam D. Cruz; 5t Photolibrary/Bios; 5tr Shutterstock/Michael Zysman; 5bc Shutterstock/Luis Cesar Tejo; 5br Shutterstock/Peter Betts; 6bl Shutterstock/Johan Swanepoel; 6tr Getty/Gerald Hinde/Gallo Images; 6br Naturepl/Andy Rouse; 7tl Frank Lane Picture Agency (FLPA)/David Hosking; 7tc Shutterstock/fivespots; 7tr Shutterstock/mikeledray; 7ct Photolibray/digital vision; 7c FLPA/Suzi Eszterhas; 7cb Photolibrary/digital vision; 7bl Naturepl/Andy Rouse; 7cr Shutterstock/Ecoprint; 7br Shutterstock/Daniel Alvarez; 8bl Shutterstock/Daniel Alvarez; 8tr Naturepl/Carline Schrurs; 8br Photolibrary/Ingram Publishing; 9tl Alamy/blinkwinkel; 9tr Shutterstock/Ewan Cheser; 9ct Shutterstock/Daniel Alvarez; 9c Alamy/Image Source; 9cb Alamy/Malcolm Schyul; 9cr Shutterstock/Brian Becker; 9bl FLPA/Suzi Eszterhas; 9br Shutterstock/Ecoprint; 9br Shutterstock/jannoon028; 10bl Shutterstock/Ecoprint; 10tr FLPA/Suzi Eszterhas; 10br Getty/Anup Shah; 11tl Photolibrary/Imagebroker; 11tr Shutterstock/Denis Donohue; 11ct Photolibrary/Creatas; 11c Shutterstock/Peter Betts; 11cb Shutterstock/jg1247; 11bc Shutterstock/Jeff Schultes; 11bl Photolibrary/Peter Arnold Images; 11cr Alamy/Jonathan Plant; 11br Shutterstock/Apirut; 12bl Alamy/Jonathan Plant; 13tl Shutterstock/Steffen Foerster; 13tr Shutterstock/Sam D. Cruz; 13ct Photolibrary/Werner Bollmann; 13c Alamy/RHPL; 13cb Photolibrary/OSF; 13cr Shutterstock/Johan Swanepoel; 13br Shutterstock/Olena Kucherenko; 14bl FLPA/Imagebroker; 15tr Shutterstock/Manamana; 15ct FLPA/Imagebroker; 15c FLPA/Imagebroker; 15cb FLPA/Imagebroker; 15cr Naturepl/Stefan Widstrand; 15br Shutterstock/cameilia; 15bc Shutterstock/Roger Meerts; 16bl Alamy/Imagebroker; 16tr Shutterstock/Worakit Sirijinda; 16br Photolibrary/Peter Arnold Images; 17tl Photolibrary/OSF; 17tr Shutterstock/Marek Mierzejewski; 17ct Shutterstock/Worakit Sirijinda; 17c Naturepl/Peter Bassett; 17cb Shutterstock/Alfredo Cerra; 17bc Shutterstock/Jens Stott; 17bl Photolibrary/Markus Botzek; 17cr Alamy/Lonely Planet; 17br Shutterstock/Borislav Gnjidic; 18bl Alamy/Lonely Planet; 18tr Photolibrary/Animals Animals; 18br Alamy/Corbis; 19tl Photolibrary/All Canada Photos; 19tr Shutterstock/Christian Mokri; 19ct Shutterstock/Geoffrey Kuchera; 19c Photolibrary/All Canada Photos; 19cb Shutterstock/S. R. Maglione; 19bl Photolibrary/OSF; 19cr Shutterstock/Ronnie Howard; 19br Shutterstock/dabjola; 20bl Alamy/All Canada Photos; 20tr Corbis/W. Perry Conway; 20br Corbis/W. Perry Conway; 21tl FLPA/Jim Brandenburg/Minden; 21tr Shutterstock/Brenda Carson; 21ct Naturepl/David Kjaer; 21c Alamy/Hornbil Images; 21cb Shutterstock/Geanina Bechea; 21bc Shutterstock/Stephen Mcsweeny; 21bl Alamy/Arco Images GmbH; 21br Shutterstock/Ambient Ideas; 22bl Photolibrary; Barbara Magnusson; 22tr Photolibrary/Juniors Bildarchiv; 23tc Shutterstock/Melinda Fawver; 23tr Shutterstock/Alex Kuzovlev; 23ct Photolibrary/All Canada Photos; 23c Alamy/Steve Amblin; 23cb Photolibrary/All Canada Photos; 23cr Shutterstock/Apirut; 24bl Alamy/Michelle Gilders; 25tr Naturepl/Tom Vezo; 24br Ardea/Francois Gohier; 25tl Corbis/W. Perry Conway; 25tc Shutterstock/Larsek; 25tr Shutterstock/Norman Bateman; 25ct FLPA/Michael Quinton; 25c Photolibrary/Animals Animals; 25cb Photolibrary/Superstock; 25bl Alamy/Visual & Written SL; 25br Shutterstock/Elena Elisseva; 25br Shutterstock/Le Do; 26bl Photolibrary/Charles Volkland; 26tr Photolibrary/Animals Animals; 26br FLPA/Donald M. Jones/Minden; 27tl Photolibrary/Animals Animals; 27tr Shutterstock/pix2go; 27ct Shutterstock/Geoffrey Kuchera; 27c Photolibrary/Animals Animals; 27cb FLPA/Sumio Harada/Minden; 27cr Shutterstock/Xico Putini; 27bl Photolibrary/Animals Animals; 27br Shutterstock/Gerald A. De Boer; 27br Shutterstock/Mark Herreid; 30tl Shutterstock/alslutsky; 30bl Shutterstock/Yuri Bershadsky; 30tr Shutterstock/Yuri Bershadsky; 31tl Shutterstock/Jens Stott; 31tr Shutterstock/Judy Whitton; 31bc Shutterstock/Manamana; 31br Shutterstock/Yuri Bershadsky; 32tl Shutterstock/Larsek; 32br Shutterstock/Mogens Trolle

Contents

Introduction

Grasslands are large areas of grasses and plants, sometimes with a few trees. They have different names in different parts of the world, including prairies, pampas, steppes, plains, and savanna.

All animals must eat to live. They hunt for food and try not to be eaten by predators. The list of who eats who is called a food chain.

Animals that eat plants are called consumers because they eat other living things. These include kangaroo, bison, elephants, and many others, such as tiny insects.

NORTH AMERICA

prairies

equator

SOUTH AMERICA

pampas

Most food chains start with plants like this wild grass. They are called producers because they make their own food from the energy of the Sun.

4

The next animal in a food chain eats small, slow prey. This lizard from the African savanna, for example, eats insects, mammals, eggs, birds, and dead animal remains.

This book follows three food chains in grasslands around the world. You will learn about the life cycles of 11 animals: how they are born, grow, reproduce, and die and what, if anything, eats them.

EUROPE

steppes

ASIA

AFRICA

plains

savanna

AUSTRALIA

At the top of a food chain is a top predator, such as a lion. Top predators are big, strong, and fast, and no other animal can catch them.

Zebra

Zebras roam the African savanna in huge herds, eating grasses and plants. Their striped skin makes it difficult for predators to pick out a single animal in a herd.

1 Males fight to take young females, called mares, from other zebra families. They want to have a group of females, called a harem, to mate with.

2 Twelve months after mating, a female gives birth to a single foal. It can stand and walk almost right away and can run on its long legs after an hour.

4 A zebra family is made up of a male, or stallion, up to six mares, and their foals. Families join together to form herds. One animal in each family stays awake at night to guard the herd.

3 The foal suckles milk from its mother for up to 16 months, although it also eats grass.

Did you know?

No two zebras look the same. Each stripe pattern is different, like a human fingerprint. The skin is black underneath the white stripes.

When its ears stand up, a zebra is happy. When they point forward, it is interested or afraid, and when they are laid back, it is angry.

Zebras eat almost all the time. Their food is tough, so it is difficult for them to get the nutrients from it.

Zebras can live for 20 years. They are usually safe in their herd, but danger lurks in the long grass for a lone zebra . . .

Hyena

Hyenas work together to hunt grazing animals, such as zebras. They live in groups, or clans, of about 80 animals. They are good swimmers and sometimes hide their kill in the water.

1 Hyena clans live in burrows dug by other animals. Three or four months after mating, a female gives birth to two cubs.

2 The cubs have soft black fur, but they are not cute and cuddly. They have long, sharp teeth, and sometimes one cub will attack and kill the other one.

8

4 The cubs have their spotted adult coats by three months old, and they start to hunt by the age of one. Females stay with the clan, but males leave when they are two years old.

3 Newborn hyenas feed about six times a day. Milk is their only food for the first eight months, and they will continue to suckle until they are one year old.

Did you know?

A hyena's bite is so strong that it can crunch through bone. Hyenas eat every part of the animals they catch, even hooves and horns.

A hyena can eat one-third of its body weight in one meal.

Hyenas have much better eyesight than humans. They can find their prey easily, even when they hunt at night.

Hyenas live for about 12 years, but bigger animals often steal their food and sometimes kill them . . .

Lion

Lions are the top hunters of the
African savanna, with a diet
of zebras and wildebeests. They
often steal prey from hyenas
and cheetahs and will kill
them if they try to fight back.

1 About four months after mating,
a female gives birth to a litter of up
to six cubs. Their eyes do not open for
a week. Their coats are spotted until
they are three months old.

2 The mother hides her young cubs
from the other lions in her group,
called the pride. Every few weeks,
she carries them to a new den.

4 A pride of lions has one or two males, five or six females, and their cubs. Females are smaller and faster, so they do the hunting. Most males leave the pride at 2—3 years old.

3 After about seven months, the cubs stop suckling and start to eat meat. They join in the hunt when they are one year old.

Did you know?

Lions rub their heads together when they meet. Males mostly greet males; females and cubs say hello to females.

A male lion has a shaggy mane that helps him look big, strong, and healthy. It grows darker as he gets older.

A male lion's roar can be heard 5 miles (8km) away. It scares rivals and tells the pride where he is.

Male lions live for 10—12 years, females for 15 years. No animals eat them, but some need them for food . . .

Vulture

Vultures are the scavengers of the savanna. They eat prey that other animals, such as lions, have killed and left behind. They help keep the savanna clean by eating flesh that would otherwise lie and rot.

1 A pair of vultures makes a wide nest of sticks lined with grass high up in a tall tree. Here, the female lays a single egg. There could be six nests in a single tree.

2 Both parents help keep the egg warm for about 56 days until it hatches. Then the female stays with her chick for three weeks while the male gets food for the whole family.

4 Sometimes hundreds of adult vultures eat an animal together. They can do this because each type of vulture eats a different part of the dead animal.

White-backed vultures have short feathers on their heads. Longer feathers would get very messy when the vultures eat.

A vulture's beak is hooked to grip and pull at flesh. African white-backed vultures feed on the soft parts of a carcass and cannot bite through thick skin.

3 Each parent stores food in a pouch in its neck, called a crop. It brings up, or regurgitates, the food for its chick. The crop holds a lot of food, so the parents do not have to leave the nest often.

Vultures glide high up in the sky on big, broad wings that catch the hot air rising from the savanna.

Vultures live for about 18 years. They are rarely attacked by other animals.

Grasshopper

Grasshoppers are insects and eat plants. Some are green, so they are hidden in the undergrowth. Others are brightly colored to warn predators that they could be harmful. They live all over the world, including on the pampas of South America.

1 In the summer, females lay batches of 20–35 eggs in the ground, covered in frothy foam that protects them while they grow.

2 The eggs stay in the ground for up to nine months. When the weather becomes warm in the spring, the eggs hatch and nymphs tunnel up to the surface.

4 Grasshoppers stay in one place for as long as there is enough food. When they have eaten it all, they move on.

3 It takes 45 days for the nymphs to become adults. They shed their skin five times as they grow. They develop wings, too, but these are small and are not used for flying.

Did you know?

Grasshoppers have powerful mouthparts, or mandibles, that move sideways to cut and chew leaves and stems.

Male grasshoppers rub their long hind legs against their wings to make clicking sounds to attract mates.

Grasshoppers have two main eyes, made of thousands of tiny lenses, and three smaller eyes.

Adult grasshoppers may live for only about three months because they are gobbled up by many animals . . .

Rhea

Rheas cannot fly, but they can run and fight. These huge birds roam the treeless pampas, eating plants, seeds and fruit, small lizards, and grasshoppers.

1 A male rhea scrapes a nest out of the ground with his feet and beak. He then attracts a female to mate with by running toward her with his wings stretched out.

2 After mating, the female lays up to ten eggs. The male will try to attract more females to mate with. Rhea nests can hold 30–60 eggs from up to ten different females.

4 The male protects the chicks fiercely, and they grow to half their adult size in six months. They can breed from the age of two.

3 The male looks after the eggs on his own for about five weeks. The first chick calls from inside its egg, and all the chicks break out of their shells within 36 hours.

Did you know?

Rheas are good fighters. They use their three-toed feet to kick enemies, such as rival birds, when they fight.

Rheas lay many eggs. This makes it more likely that some will survive if the nest is attacked by a predator.

When a rhea eats, it grabs food in its beak and lifts up its head. The food can then slip down its long neck into its stomach.

Rheas can live for up to 15 years unless they meet an animal with faster legs and big jaws . . .

Cougar

Cougars, or pumas, are cats with very powerful jaws. They can grab and eat almost any animal they come across in their territory, including deer, other mammals, birds, and insects.

1 Three months after mating, the female gives birth to two or three cubs. The young live on their mother' milk for seven weeks.

2 Cougar cubs have spotted coats with black rings around their tails. Their eyes are blue but turn amber or green as the cubs grow.

Adult cougars measure about 8 feet (2.4m) from nose to tail and weigh about 155 pounds (70kg).

3 The mother shows the cubs where she has killed prey, and they play fight to practice their hunting kills. After six months, they begin to hunt small animals on their own.

Did you know?

Cougars have razor-sharp claws that pull in when they are not needed so they do not get dull.

A cougar has powerful legs. It can leap 10 feet (3m) up in the air and sprint at up to 30 miles per hour (50km/h).

The cougar's very long, black-tipped tail helps it keep its balance as it turns, leaps, and chases prey.

Cougars can live for 10–12 years. They may have rival hunters, but no other animal is likely to kill them.

Prairie dog

Prairie dogs are not dogs! In fact, they are squirrels that live in underground burrows and eat grasses and weeds growing on North American prairies.

1 In January, a female mates with several males, so the three or four pups born about 30 days later can have different fathers. The pups are born blind and hairless.

2 The pups stay in the burrow for five weeks and do not even open their eyes. They suckle milk from their mother.

4 Prairie dog families are made up of one male, two to eight females, and their young. They live close together in underground "towns" linked by tunnels.

3 After about six weeks, they start to eat grass outside the burrow. They also explore nearby burrows and meet other families in the colony.

Did you know?

When prairie dogs meet, they touch their front teeth together. This shows that they know each other and looks as if they are kissing!

Prairie dogs pile up soil at the burrow entrance. They sit on this mound to watch for approaching attackers.

Prairie dogs are so called because they bark like dogs. They make a different bark for each different type of predator.

Prairie dogs live for five to seven years, but other animals try to take over their burrows— and sometimes eat them . . .

Rattlesnake

Prairie rattlesnakes like to live in underground dens. As they cannot dig, they take over the burrows of tunneling animals such as prairie dogs. They eat them, too, if they can.

1 Rattlesnakes hibernate from October to March, and then they mate. Six months later, several females give birth to their live young in a shared den.

2 Between four and 12 young are born. The number of babies depends on how much food there was for the mother in the previous year. A lot of food means a lot of babies.

4 Prairie rattlesnakes shed their skin up to five times in the first year and several more times after that. With each shedding, an extra "bead" forms in the rattle.

3 The young snakes have fangs and venom, but they do not yet have a rattle on the end of their tail. This starts to grow after seven days, when they first shed their skin.

Did you know?

When it is threatened, a rattlesnake lifts up its tail and shakes the rattle to make a buzzing warning sound.

Rattlesnakes kill their prey by biting them with their two venom-filled fangs. The fangs fold back into the mouth when not in use.

Snakes smell with their forked tongues, which flick in and out at all times to "taste" the air.

Rattlesnakes live for up to 20 years. Their bite and venom scare away some predators, but others can fight back . . .

American badger

American badgers are very good at digging. They make burrows to sleep in during the day, and at night they dig again to hunt for prey, such as mice and birds. They are tough fighters and will attack rattlesnakes.

1 A female badger gathers grass and takes it to a special large, deep den where she will give birth to her babies.

2 A litter of about three cubs is born in the early spring. They are blind and suckle their mother's milk for the first two to three months.

4 After about six months, the cubs leave the den to find their own territories, or ranges. Adult badgers may dig up to 10 feet (3m) into the ground each day.

3 The cubs start to explore outside the den when they are five to six weeks old. Around this time, they also begin to eat solid food.

Did you know?

Badgers use their long, powerful front claws to dig up soil and their back legs to push it away behind them.

Badgers have 34 teeth, including four longer, sharp canine teeth for holding prey. They show their teeth when they are threatened.

A badger's silvery fur is tough but loose, which makes it difficult for snakes to bite through to the flesh.

American badgers live for five to ten years. Above the ground, they are in danger from quick-footed predators . . .

Coyote

Coyotes hunt alone or in packs. They sometimes hunt alongside badgers, but they will eat them, too, especially the young. Coyotes are omnivores, so they eat fruit and vegetables as well as meat.

1 About two months after mating, a female gives birth to a litter of about six pups. Their eyes open when they are ten days old.

2 The pups suckle their mother's milk and are able to leave the den when they are one month old.

4 The pups are fully grown in a year, and the males leave. A coyote pack is made up of six related adults and their young.

3 Within five weeks, they start eating solid food. The parents cough up, or regurgitate, half-eaten food for them and bring live mice to the den so that the pups can learn how to hunt.

Did you know?

Coyotes stalk their prey using their strong sense of smell. It also helps them find dead animals to eat.

Their tails point down when they run but get more bushy if they are alarmed and want to look bigger and more fierce.

Coyotes grow thick winter coats that they shed during the warmer summer months.

Coyotes live for about ten years. Pups often die young, but adults have very few predators and are at the top of many food chains.

A North American prairie food web

This book follows some grassland food
chains. Most animals eat more than one
food, however, so they are part of several
food chains. There are many food
chains in the grasslands, and
they link like a map to
make a food web.

golden
eagle

snake

coyote

badger

toad

mouse

leaves

prairie dog

beetle

seeds

Sun

bird

grasshopper

fruit

Glossary

AMBER
A deep yellow color.

BURROW
A hole or tunnel in the ground where an animal lives.

CANINE TEETH
Special long, pointed teeth used for cutting through food.

CARCASS
The body of a dead animal.

COLONY
A group of the same kind of animals that live together.

CONSUMER
A living thing that survives by eating other living things.

DEN
A wild animal's home.

FANGS
Long, pointed teeth. Snake fangs can inject venom.

FLESH
The soft parts of the body between the skin and the bones.

FOAL
A young horse, donkey, or zebra.

GLIDE
To fly without flapping the wings.

HIBERNATE
When an animal rests through the winter.

LITTER
A group of baby animals born to the same mother.

MAMMAL
An animal that has fur and feeds its young on milk.

MATE
When a male and female animal reproduce. For some animals, there is a particular time each year when they mate, and this is called the mating season.

MOUND
A pile of soil.

OMNIVORE
An animal that eats plants and other animals.

PAMPAS
A huge area of grassy plains in South America.

PRAIRIE
A large area of flat land that does not get much rain.

PREDATOR
An animal that kills and eats other animals.

PREY
An animal hunted by a predator.

PRODUCER
A living thing, such as a plant, that makes its own food from the energy of the Sun.

RIVAL
Two animals are rivals when they both want the same thing.

SAVANNA
A large plain covered with tall grasses.

SHEDDING
When an animal gets rid of the outside of its body. This is also called molting.

SPRINT
To run fast over a short distance.

STALK
To creep up on prey.

SUCKLE
When a baby animal drinks milk from its mother.

TERRITORY
An area of land where one animal or group of animals lives and hunts.

UNDERGROWTH
The low-growing plants and shrubs in a forest.

VENOM
A liquid injected by an animal to kill its prey.

These websites have information about grasslands or their animals—or both!

- chalk.richmond.edu/education/projects/webunits/ biomes/grass.html
- environment.nationalgeographic.com/ environment/habitats/grassland-profile
- factzoo.com
- kidcyber.com.au/topics/animals.htm
- kidsgeo.com/geography-for-kids
- kids.nationalgeographic.com/kids

Index